BOOK DESCRIPTION

How to Master Small Talk is a practical and easy-to-read guide for people who would like to learn the art of small talk and become more confident, likeable, and outgoing individuals. Small talk, although seemingly superficial, is an integral part of everyone's lives. We all need to make small talk once in a while, and it's not so easy for most of us. We all need to put some effort into making small talk, especially with people we don't know well. Mastering small talk requires some skill and practice, which is why this book was written.

After reading this book, you will gain a broader perspective about people in general. The more you begin to appreciate everyone you meet in your everyday life, the easier it will be for you to master the skill of small talk. You will learn what makes some people nervous while talking to others, and how they can overcome it, ways to remember things to say, and lots of tips and tricks so as to never run out of interesting conversation ideas.

The essence of *How To Master Small Talk* is to help you understand your own value as an individual. You have the ability to conquer anything and be the most charismatic person you could ever be!

HOW TO MASTER SMALL TALK

How to Be Confident, Outgoing, Likeable, and Never Run Out of Things to Say

Danny Carlson

Table Of Contents

References

Introduction

Making small talk is not everyone's cup of tea, and that's totally okay! We are all unique beings with our own set of traits, strengths, abilities, and limitations. Some of us are able to make small talk with effortless candor; in fact, some of us like to indulge in it whenever possible–"Oh, you look so pretty in this dress! It looks so summery and nice. I also wanted something like this for myself," "Can I help you with your bags?" "I'd like to buy a new phone. Can you suggest which one I should go for?"

However, for some people, it's a big task to make small talk. Most of us keep quiet if there's apparently no need to talk. There are many situations where we could break the ice, but instead we choose to remain silent. Why does that happen? Well, many of us don't feel the need to talk or speak without reason. We talk only when someone asks us a question, or if we need to ask something.

Life is filled with many instances, occasions, events, and circumstances; as human beings, we need to be communicative to be able to associate with other people. For instance: You have moved to a new house, and your next-door neighbor invites you for a cup of coffee. Wouldn't you want to go, sit, and chat? Maybe or maybe not.

Life continues to throw moments and opportunities your way to talk to people, know them, and be part of their lives in some way or the other. Small talk always comes in handy. We may think there's no need for small talk, but there is. Perhaps you are at a party where you don't know anybody. You see people already being buddy-buddy with each other. What would you do in a situation like that? Would you just stand in a corner with a drink, or would you go up to at least one person and start a conversation?

The key is whoever makes small talk is appreciated and accepted by others quite easily. On the other hand, those who don't engage in any small talk fizzle out from people's memories. We are social animals after all.

When you stay quiet at a social gathering, people perceive you in a certain way. They might find you snooty, boring, or a loner. Everybody needs words, thoughts, and expressions from others to feel wanted and accepted. Therefore, when there's no small talk in a given situation, people tend to feel ignored, or even rejected. So you need to step into the shoes of others and understand how they feel.

Small talk can ease a lot of things for you—it can make you a more likeable, outgoing, and confident individual. Small talk acts like a social lubricant that binds all of us. We all need each other, and small talk bridges the distance.

You may not be born with the knack of small talk; however, it's not a hard skill to learn! It's absolutely okay to be a certain way; however, it's not okay to remain stagnant throughout your life. It's beneficial to develop good habits and helpful skills, no matter how young or old you are. We learn every day. If you need to learn and imbibe a quality or skill that can bring you closer to others, and make you more amicable, then you should embrace the opportunity.

Being the kind of person who never runs out of things to say is valuable. It's good to be friendly and nice to everyone you meet. The knack of conversations can help *you* more than anybody else —people who always have something to talk about are usually happier, more energetic, and full of life. Such people extend their radiance to others as well.

Anybody can master small talk, with some thought and practice. You can find plenty of ways to remember conversation ideas, as well as use them whenever needed. You can begin by practicing small talk with the people you meet in your everyday life, as a step up to more outgoing scenarios such as parties, get-togethers, and picnics.

After having read this book, you will build the ideas and skills capable of striking conversations anywhere, with any person. You will understand that it's not really necessary to like everybody. You don't have to be in everybody's good graces, or be their best friend. You don't have to agree with everybody. You can be your own self and still be the most captivating person around!

This book will teach you the art of dealing with different people, disagreeing amicably, using the power of conversations to be endearing, and celebrating the amazing individual you were born to be.

So enjoy learning *How to Master Small Talk*!

CHAPTER 1: WHAT IS SMALL TALK AND HOW IT'S A PART OF YOUR LIFE

Small talk, by definition, is just a polite conversation over trivial matters. It's essentially a superficial way of connecting with people you meet for the first time. So, you begin with light-hearted, informal chat. You can start with something as simple as "It's pretty cold today, isn't it," then wait for the other person to respond.

You don't have to talk about something serious, or controversial. In fact, you should refrain from doing so. The beauty of small talk is, even though it's superficial in nature, it can be significant.

Your life will lose its sheen without an indulgence in occasional small talk. No matter who you are—young, old, a college student, a professional, a homemaker, or a retiree, you cannot ignore the value of small talk.

The fact that you will bump into opportunities of small talk without even trying should make you want to master it. You have to remember it's an inevitable aspect of your life, so you better embrace it, rather than try to run away from it.

How Small Talk Is Part of Your Life

Being social is one of the most essential aspects of our lives. Some people are more outgoing and have more of an active social life with many friends. They have more opportunities to exchange their thoughts and opinions. Then there are people who are not so social. They like to socialize only once in a while, as they may have their own set of things to do. So, everybody has their own preferences in regards to connecting with others. However, the fact remains that everybody has to make small talk to some degree. As mentioned earlier, you cannot avoid it completely!

The Need to Make Small Talk at Work

Maybe you are a professional who works in a big organization with a super frenzied schedule, leaving you little to no time for small talk. However, it is still very much part of your life. You cannot escape talking to your coworkers; it'll happen at least once in a while. Maybe you'll need to assist somebody at work, or maybe work under somebody else. And what about that office party? There are various possibilities where the need to make small talk does arrive.

Here are a few examples of small talk at work:

- "Could you please help me with the presentation? I am working on something like this for the first time, so I would need a little guidance on how to go about the flow of it."
- "I really appreciate your help. If you need any assistance in regards to any of your work, let me know."
- "It's getting a bit late now. I have to rush. Would you mind if we discuss this tomorrow?"

Everyday Small Talk Opportunities

People get many small talk moments in their everyday lives, too. You may bump into your neighbor while stepping out of your house, resulting in an exchange of smiles, a greeting, or some pleasantries, if not much. Maybe you'll meet an acquaintance while you're on your way to work, somebody may request you to let them get ahead at the checkout counter, or you might need to ask somebody to let you sit by the window on a bus.

Let's look at the example below where you meet your neighbor in the elevator:

"Hi, Mr. White! How's your arm now? I hope it's not so painful anymore. I remember you said you were supposed to visit a physician last Thursday."

"It's much better now. In fact, it got better without the physician's help. I just did some stretching and the pain began to subside gradually."

"That's so good to hear! I hope it gets better soon."

"Yeah, I hope so too. Thank you very much!"

Small Talk on More Important Occasions

Small talk connects all of us; nobody can do without small talk. It's even more important for bigger scenarios such as college debates, job interviews, office events, weddings, or your first date.

Making small talk is necessary whenever we meet people, especially if we meet them for the very first time. For example: You are on your first date and you want to create a great impression on the other person. You can't do it solely based on the way you are dressed or how you look. It has to be your words, body language, and smile which should make them feel comfortable.

You can begin with something simple, such as mentioning a coffee shop, "Have you been here before?" You can actually incorporate cues from what is going on around you—the atmosphere of the restaurant, the waiters, the kind of people present there, and the food and drinks served there.

You can ask your date what they would like to start with, or you can recommend something nice that you have already enjoyed (if you visit the place regularly).

Certain Unprecedented Situations

If you are forced into small talk in unavoidable situations, such as being stuck in an elevator with somebody and obviously you want to get out of it as soon as possible. You can't just keep quiet and expect something to happen on its own. The first thing you will probably do is call security. In the meantime, you may want to ask the other person if they know a way out.

Similarly, in a situation wherein you need to rush to the airport or the hospital, and you discover your car has a flat tire, you will look for instant help. You may want to ask your neighbor to drop you at the bus stop or, if you are at work, you might want to ask for help from a colleague.

Professional Networking Events

Networking is a necessary evil these days. You don't meet people for just personal friendships, but also for possible professional avenues in the future. No matter what you do for a living—work in a school, hospital, bank, or run your own business, mingling with other people has become mandatory for your success.

For instance: You are looking for a new job and there's a networking event happening at a café, and you are likely to meet people in a similar profession as yours. How would you go about striking conversations with others? You cannot simply ask somebody, "Hey, do you have a job for me?" You got to make some small talk and get them to know you first, understand a little bit about your professional background, and your personality before they consider you for a job. They might not even have a job for you. However, they might want to recommend your name to somebody who does.

In a scenario where you don't know anybody, and it's absolutely necessary for you to talk, the skill of small talk is required. You need to remove the layers of that shell around you to get to talk to people. Being coy and reserved can't help you much in such scenarios.

CHAPTER 2: WHY DO SOME PEOPLE FEEL NERVOUS WHILE TALKING TO OTHERS

Do you feel anxious, self-conscious, or awkward while talking to somebody? Are you someone who just waits for the conversation to end? If your answer is yes, this chapter is for you.

There are people who feel nervous while talking to others and there are various layers and reasons why. According to psychologists and mental health experts, if a person feels an intense level of anxiety about meeting new people, or talking to people, it is called social anxiety disorder (SAD), though there are varying degrees to it; we can't put everyone in the same box and jump to conclusions about a person's anxiety.

Anyone can feel nervous or shy about talking to others because of varying and complex reasons. However, there is nothing we cannot solve or overcome. Each person has the ability to subdue their own weaknesses. It's a matter of digging deep into what makes you stay away from conversations and dealing with them head-on.

Let's look at the hindrances keeping people from making small talk:

Thoughts and Opinions About

Themselves and Others

It's one's self-consciousness that makes you feel shy or anxious. There are people who constantly think about how other people perceive them. Such people have a low opinion of themselves. They feel whatever they are going to say might not sound right. They are always conscious about what opinion others will form about them.

They analyze themselves a bit too much. Therefore, such people avoid getting into conversations, especially with new people.

For instance, when a self-conscious person enters a room full of people, they feel like hiding under a table and not being seen. Such a feeling emerges from their wrong way of thinking, feeling as if everybody is constantly looking at them.

Upbringing, Family Background, and Cultural Norms

Some people feel nervous about talking to others because of personal backgrounds and the environment they grew up in. For instance, someone may find it hard to be outgoing if they come from an extremely closeted family background. There are families where children were not given enough freedom to shape into the kind of personality they were meant to be.

A person's childhood has a great impact on their behavior and mental wellbeing. Some people face many harsh criticisms as a child by their own parents, relatives, and teachers, causing them to grow into a shy person.

Some people are able to overcome their shyness, only growing up and meeting people who make them feel good about themselves. For instance, if they make friends with others or get in a relationship during their college years, they have a chance to discover who they are and develop more confidence.

Not Being Confident in the Language

Sometimes people don't want to engage in a conversation because of their inability to speak fluently in a particular language. They have a constant fear of making mistakes while talking, and being ridiculed about it. Such hesitation could have emerged out of past experiences. They might have been jeered by people for speaking certain words in a certain way.

The Shy Nature of a Person

It's natural for shy people to find it difficult to talk to others. Shyness could be genetic, or it could be a person's personality. There's nothing strange or wrong about it. Different personality types have different approaches toward being social. However, shyness should not act as a roadblock in your journey of building relationships—personal or professional. Some people allow their shyness to rule them, which is not right.

Shy people often miss out on relationships and many significant opportunities in life. Communication is the key to solving most problems, which is why shyness is not a great virtue to have.

Being Too Conscious of Superficial Factors

Most people who are nervous about talking to others are more anxious about how they appear, their clothes, body language, and style of talking. They give too much importance to their flaws. For instance, a person who stutters while talking could feel self-conscious when speaking.

People also refrain from being social when they are constantly teased about the way they look, especially by their own parents, siblings, or extended family members. Most people develop their self-image based on what they have been told by other people.

Being Lazy and Self-Centered

Some people are simply lazy and don't want to make the effort of connecting with new people and making friends. They like to keep to themselves and be busy with their own things. They aren't really anxious or nervous while talking to people, but they generally don't like to talk. Such personalities might be thought of as snooty. However, they are just being themselves.

Now that we have discussed a few root causes of people being nervous while talking, let's look at some of the practical solutions to them as well.

Accept Your Anxiety

The first step toward dealing with your anxiety is to accept it. Don't hide or ignore it. Don't be bogged down by it. The moment you accept it, you will feel lighter and find it much easier to overcome it.

In fact, take your shyness in your stride. Know that there are many people like you who feel just as you do. Nervousness or shyness can be overcome easily with self-motivation, ideas, and practice.

Take Small Steps Toward Talking to Others

Begin by taking small steps instead of trying to be outgoing at parties and weddings. Resolve to initiate small talk with people you meet in your everyday life—the paperboy, housekeepers, dog walkers, and your fellow passengers on trains and buses. The benefit of talking to such people who are not related to you, but they come in contact with you every day, is that they are not going to judge you. They have no preconceived notions about you. So, you have the opportunity to discover your own wit and knack of repartee with them.

Enjoy Being Yourself

The key to confidence is being who you are and not trying to imitate somebody else. It's important to stay relaxed and enjoy your own uniqueness. Don't stifle your own growth as an individual by evaluating who you are according to world standards. Don't think too much; just lighten up a bit and allow yourself to be who you truly are.

Stay Around Positive People

Be sure to stick to positive, helpful, and friendly people. Also, be sure to stay away from negative people. Positive people will encourage you, show you the right way, and be part of your life. Surrounding yourself with positive people will bring out the best in you. You will soon realize you are a beautiful person and begin to feel more confident about yourself.

Talk to Somebody About Your Nervousness

It's always good to talk to somebody about your problems. If you think you need a professional coach, talk to them. Make sure you bare your heart to somebody who you trust, but is also older, more mature, and much more learned than you. It's not so important what they tell you to do, but rather just the act of speaking to them.

Believe You Are a Confident, Smart, and Kind Person

Remember, there's nobody who knows you better than yourself. Think of yourself as somebody who's confident, smart, and kind. The more you condition yourself into believing, the easier it will be for you to deal with shyness or anxiety.

Practice smiling and talking to people in front of your mirror; doing this every day will help ensure you get it right.

Feeling nervous around others or getting cold feet while talking can be an issue for many people. However, it can be overcome with self realization, positive company, and lots of time spent practicing small talk.

CHAPTER 3: THE PURPOSE OF SMALL TALK IN YOUR LIFE

Small talk plays a potent role in our lives. It's usually associated with talking to people who you are not too familiar with or complete strangers, and may sound frivolous. You may not realize the importance of small talk because it's so simple. It fits into our lives with such ease that we take it for granted.

All the serious, important, and deep things in life begin with small talk. Whether it's going in for a job interview, your first date, meeting a client for business, buying a property, or visiting a doctor, every occasion has small talk involved on some level. It's an integral part of everyone's life. Even the most purposeless small talk lasting barely five minutes can brighten up someone's day— a simple compliment about someone's new hair style, a listening ear to someone's problem at work, or a quick check on someone's health all add so much joy to one's life.

Small talk is like testing the waters before diving in. When you meet somebody for the first time, you don't know them at all, which is why you don't jump into serious or personal topics immediately. To share something intimate with someone, you need to trust them. A deep, long-lasting friendship with someone blossoms after many inconsequential talks -

"Beautiful weather, isn't it?

"How has your day been?"

"Oh, I had better days?"

"I love that bar down the street. Have you been there?"

"Yeah, I'd love to check that out!"

"How long have you been living here?"

"I didn't like it much. What do you think?"

Small talk is the beginning of so many beautiful relationships, and so many other big personal and professional endeavors.

Let's look closely at how small talk impacts your life.

Builds Your Social Life

Small talk is a social glue that cements relationships. All the aimless chatter and banter leads to building up your social life. You get many opportunities to know different people; their quirks add a dash of energy in your life, and that's how you build connections over a period of time.

Social life is essential for your mental and emotional wellbeing. You don't have to be excessively social or be friends with everybody you meet. However, you need to have at least a few good friends to count on.

People perceive you in a certain way when you don't make any effort at small talk. You might come across as someone who is not interested in being social. On the contrary, when you make small talk efforts, people tend to like you and want to hang out with you. They find you more approachable.

Helps You Cultivate Better Relationships

People who engage in small talk with most people they meet end up fostering better relationships. You may say certain things with a genuine and meaningful intent and not just for effect. You can show your sincere concern toward someone's crisis. You don't have to simply remark, "Oh, I am so sorry to hear that." You can also be empathetic and say something like, "I understand it's tough for you. Can I be of some help?"

Small talk is not just meant to avoid silences or kill time. It can be an expression of comfort that you want to give someone who might need it. That's how people remember you for who you are—they like you and acknowledge your kindness.

Some relationships are purely based on small talk made over the years, such as your friendship with your neighbors. The tradition of making eye contact and smiling at your neighbor every morning when you water your plants, asking them how they are doing, making a remark at how beautiful their little garden has turned out, goes a long way.

If you happen to need your neighbor's help in any matter, it's a little awkward to knock on their doors without any foundation of small talk in the past. So, small talk is like building blocks that lead to something more fruitful and rewarding later.

You Live a More Satisfying Life

People who have great conversational skills connect better with all kinds of personalities. They know the knack of cajoling even the introverts into stimulating conversations. You live a more wholesome and satisfying life when you use your small talk ability to the fullest, and let other people feel more wanted and appreciated.

You can be the listening ear to somebody else; encourage them, build their confidence by making them feel good about themselves. Small talk is a great technique to lighten up a situation, ease someone's anxiety, and make them feel comfortable.

You Can Build Solid Professional Connections

We all know small talk opens doors for new work opportunities. However, we still shy away from making that small effort, right? Well, we need to be in front of many people to be able to find that perfect job. Building a career is not just about going for interviews or slogging at your current job. To find the right opportunities, you need to meet different people from time to time. Therefore, you need to attend all sorts of professional networking events, and make yourself visible to people by making small talk.

Your potential employer might like you over other contenders for the way you made small talk and gave them a few insights into your personality, rather than just showing them your resume.

Small talk should be used as a smart tool to secure prolific, professional relationships.

CHAPTER 4: SMALL TALK IDEAS TO KEEP HANDY

The best way to never run out of things to say is to always know in advance what to talk about. Keeping small talk ideas in mind can be helpful in making sure you never draw a blank in any given scenario. There are occasions you can be well-prepared for—new guests coming over your place, you visiting someone for the first time, or attending an event where you will be meeting many new people.

So what are those enticing conversation ideas? What should you really talk about when you meet someone for the first time? Well, there are many things you can talk about. However, you should focus only on the simple stuff. Don't stress over it. Don't take it as a task. Rather, you should enjoy it and look forward to it.

How to Never Run Out of Things to Say

The first step toward making small talk in a given scenario is being interested in meeting people, being keen on knowing them. So stop focusing on yourself and be genuinely curious to know the other person.

Ask Open-Ended Questions

You should always try to ask questions which can initiate a conversation. Avoid asking anything that has just a 'yes' or 'no' for an answer. You can start by asking "How was your weekend?" if you are meeting on a Monday. After you have asked your first question, simply wait for the other person to talk. You can take the chat forward by asking "Where did you go?" if you feel the person is interested in sharing all the details of their weekend.

You can begin by asking close-ended questions, but you should quickly jump to open-ended questions, such as "What do you do for a living?" and "How did you know what to pursue?"

Give Compliments

Say something nice about the person. It could be about their clothes, accessories, or hairstyle. Compliments can melt the ice easily and set the right direction for the conversation. However, be careful what you say. Don't be too blatant with compliments. It should be genuine and precise, far from shallow words.

Notice Something Unique About the Other Person

Being observant while meeting a new person is also helpful. You should notice something unique about the person—maybe a tattoo on their arm or a unique piece of jewelry you haven't seen before. Making a remark on something noticeable about the other person will put the ball in their court. You can stay quiet and simply listen to what they say.

Ask for Advice

You should also look for ways to seek some kind of advice from the other person. Since everybody loves to offer advice, it's a good way to persuade someone into talking. However, you should make sure you listen to their advice sincerely, not just for the sake of listening. When you listen to someone with sincere intent, it motivates the other person to connect to you better.

Talk About a Current Topic

Mention any current topic and wait for the other person to respond to it as enthusiastically as you. Allow the other person to share their views and take the conversation ahead. For instance, you mention the latest sports event that is happening in the city and how excited you are about it. Wait for the other person to show their enthusiasm, too. Don't keep blabbering when you see the other person is not so zealous about it. You may put them off by doing so. If you feel the topic is of no interest to the other, look around and mention something about the place and the surroundings, or offer to grab a drink.

Don't Change Topics Too Quickly

When you sense a conversation is flowing smoothly on a topic, don't change it too quickly. The smartest approach to staying in a conversation is to explore different aspects of it, not switching to a new topic. There's nothing better than to keep talking on a topic that stimulates both parties.

Small Talk Topic Ideas to Remember

If you are someone who always wonders what to talk about when you meet someone new, you should keep some conversation starters handy.

You Can Start by Asking About Their Job

The first thing that you can ask a new person is about their job, or what they do for a living. After they have answered the question, you can ask them what they like the most about their job, which will nudge them to talk at length. You can simply listen, nod occasionally, or add your inputs wherever appropriate. As you realize the person has finished talking, you can begin to share something about your work life.

Talk About the Current Place and Environment

Another thing you can discuss is the current place you both are at. For instance, if you are meeting at a common friend's farmhouse, talk about the beauty of the place. You can ask or mention things like -

"Have you been here before?"

"How do you like this place?"

"I like this place a lot. Even though it takes me an hour to drive here, I like coming here every once in a while."

Talk About the Weather

If you are absolutely clueless about how to begin a conversation, talk about the weather. It may be the easiest way to move on to other topics. You can say things like -

"It's so nice and sunny today!" "I like breezy summers over dreaded winters. How about you?"

"Do you enjoy spending a lazy summer afternoon in a hammock?" "What else do you like to do to unwind?"

Ask About Their Native Place

You can ask where the person comes from—their native place. It's one of the easiest conversation starters, and it engages the other person quite well. People usually enjoy talking about the city or town they were born in, or the place where they grew up. Try to mention something really nice about their city, such as, "One of my friends also comes from Boston. They told me it's a city full of energy and lots of cultural events happening all through the year. I never got a chance to experience it myself, though. But I'd love to."

Make Sure to Give Compliments

Make sure to give at least one compliment to the other person for something nice that they have—the way they are dressed, their shoes, bags, or accessories. Say things like -

"What a pretty pair of earrings you are wearing! Where did you get them from?" "I like your watch. I think I meant to buy something similar, but then I ended up buying another brand."

Exchange Shopping Advice

Right after showering some compliments, ask for some shopping advice and also share your own experiences.

"Where do you typically shop from?"

"Do you like shopping online or do you prefer to shop from physical stores?

"Yeah I like their products, too." "I find it a bit expensive, though."

Ask About Their Favorite Pastime

After you have chatted a bit about work, shopping, and life in general, ask them about their favorite pastime, the things that really energize them.

"What do you do after work hours?"

"Do you read?" "What's the latest book on your bedside?"

"Do you go out quite often?"

"How do you like to spend your weekends?"

Move On to Topics Like Movies, Music, Sports, and Travel

The best way to keep the momentum of a conversation is by continuing to add related topics to it. For instance, after you have chatted a bit about your favorite pastime, steer toward possible topics like sports, movies, music, art, food, or travel depending on what pastime you discuss.

"Do you enjoy outdoor sports?"

"Don't you think Avengers: Endgame was a bit of a drag?"

"Are you a foodie?" "What's your favorite restaurant in town?"

"Mountains or beaches?" "What's your favorite place in the world?"

Talk About Technology

You can also initiate a conversation by asking about the latest mobile phone they have. Talk a bit about how cool technology is these days, and how easy it is to do so much from one place. You can say things like -

"What's the model of your phone?" "Ah nice! It gives the best picture quality. I also want to buy this one."

You may start your small talk with any topic. There's no rule book. You just have to make sure you don't say anything to upset the other person, and the best way to deal with it is to understand cues. Build your topics based on what the other person enjoys talking about. We will also look into what you should avoid talking about later in the book.

CHAPTER 5: HOW TO BE A LIKEABLE, OUTGOING, AND CONFIDENT PERSON

Everybody wants to be loved for who they are. We don't want to be labeled as someone boring, timid, or unsocial, right? Well, it's okay to be who you are no matter how others perceive you. It's okay to be an introvert. It's okay not to enjoy social gatherings too much. It's okay to be engrossed in your own world. You don't have to change to be able to fit into someone else's shoes.

However, you want to be a likeable, outgoing, and confident person. How does that happen? To be someone who's admired by others, you need to develop certain qualities. Anybody can become the person they want to be. It's just a matter of self-analysis.

There are people who are never able to analyze themselves, which is why they never seem to grow. They remain the same person all their lives. To be likeable, one has to be willing to accept their flaws, be willing to change, and be open to stepping out of their comfort zone.

It's an interesting journey to work toward your own betterment as a human being. Working on yourself, for your own upliftment in regards to your emotional, mental and social well-being, goes a long way in shaping your life. So if you are someone who's conscious about being a nice, amiable, caring person, you should feel proud of yourself, and that should boost your confidence.

You can nourish your social life by imbibing certain helpful attributes.

Be a Genuine Listener

The best way to treat others is to genuinely listen to what they say. Most people fail at it. We pretend to listen, but we are preoccupied with our own thoughts. We are always in a hurry to voice our own thoughts. Don't do that! Instead, listen intently to what the other person is saying. You will be loved for doing something as simple as listening.

It's not always necessary to keep bantering to take a conversation forward. Sometimes, you just need to be all ears.

Smile and Acknowledge People

People who smile the moment they see someone are often more likeable than others. When you smile and acknowledge someone, it gives them a positive signal and they are drawn toward you.

The moment you enter a new place, make it a point to look around and observe things, people and the atmosphere. Find an opportunity to smile at someone and initiate small talk. Also, watch your body language. Loosen up a little bit, appear relaxed, and avoid looking into your phone too much.

Make an Eye Contact

Don't be someone who looks down or away while talking. It's kind of disrespectful not to look into the eyes of the person you are talking to. Looking into the eyes is part of connecting with a person. That's how you extend warmth, understanding, and respect to the other person.

Another point to keep in mind is to address people by their first names. Always mention the other person's name while talking to them so they feel acknowledged and accepted.

Shake Hands Warmly

Touch is an integral part of being social and human. Shake hands firmly and warmly. Avoid those cold, half-baked handshakes completely. They are a major turn off. A friendly pat on the shoulder, a warm handshake, or a hug can make the other person feel more wanted and admired.

Shaking hands also gives you the power to rule the atmosphere without dominating it.

Don't Talk Too Much About Yourself

People who talk about themselves are perceived to be self-obsessed, which is not a great quality to have. When you get into a conversation, it's a two-way deal. Thus, it can't be just about your thoughts and opinions. It has to be about the other person, too. So give the other person the first chance to speak.

Also, don't brag about yourself—what you do, the kind of money you make, your house, possessions, talents, and achievements. Instead, allow the other person to mention their big moments in life and acknowledge them.

Ask More Questions

Be genuinely interested in the other person. Show that you care to know them. Ask questions they would like to answer (refer to chapter four). However, make sure you don't sound like an interrogator. Be curious without being intrusive.

Don't ask them about their paycheck or how many social media followers they have. Ask questions based on what the other person tells you. For instance, if they tell you about their weekend plans, ask them how long they plan to stay in a place and what all activities they plan to do.

Be Around Happy, Genuine, and Friendly People

You should also learn from people who are always happy, genuinely warm, and friendly. Observe how they start a conversation, how they talk, their body language, and confidence. Try to be around them and take in some of their social skills. Positive people brush off their positivity on others, too. So let that work for you!

Be Humble, Positive, and Approachable

You will meet all sorts of people in the world. Some will be kind, warm, and friendly while some will be cold, snooty, and uncaring. The best policy is to be a humble, positive, and gentle person to everyone. You cannot change or influence someone else's behavior. But you can change your own. Kindness wins more people than anything else.

However, don't be fake. Don't pretend to like something you don't, or say things just to please somebody. The idea is to find common ground with people and stay away from topics where you have differences of opinions.

Be Aware That Everybody Has Flaws

Don't be under the false impression that everybody else except you is awesome and charismatic. That's not true at all. Just like you, even others struggle with their own set of thoughts, ideas, inhibitions, and limitations. Nobody is bothered about judging you. So you have complete freedom to be the person you would like to be.

Love Yourself

While you set out on the journey of becoming a more likeable and outgoing person, don't forget to love and celebrate yourself (more on this in the later part of the book). Remember, we all are beautiful individuals with our own share of quirks and traits. Intentionally think how confident, wonderful, and amazing you are.

To be likeable, you need to believe so first. The more you self-acknowledge your strengths, the better individual you will turn out to be.

CHAPTER 6: HOW TO DEVELOP THE KNACK FOR SMALL TALK IN YOUR EVERYDAY LIFE

If you are someone who finds it hard to enjoy small talk naturally, the easiest way to acquire the skill is by practicing it in your everyday life. The best way to overcome your shyness for small talk in more intimidating scenarios is to master it in simple, painless scenarios.

Your "everyday life" gives you plenty of opportunities to develop the knack of small talk—you can make small talk with your neighbor, mailman, gardener, chauffeur, or the cashier at the checkout counter. The idea is to make an effort in a scenario where nobody is going to judge you, or at least you won't feel you are being judged.

It's always better to start small. Give yourself easy conversation goals to achieve first. Whether you are a homemaker, an entrepreneur, or a professional who works for an organization, make it a point to connect to people whenever possible.

Talk to Everybody You Meet in a Day

Be intentional about initiating a chat with everybody you meet in a day. You don't have to say anything specific or substantial.

For instance, if you have an appointment with your doctor, take this opportunity to make polite conversation with the receptionist who has been fixing your appointments.

Ask questions or make friendly remarks, such as "How have you been?" "It looks like you have been working really hard." You can also appreciate and show them gratitude for being considerate in rescheduling your appointments whenever needed.

Try to Help People Whenever Possible

You get many opportunities to help people in some way or another through a regular day—when you are traveling on a bus and you see someone standing, you could offer them your seat. Similarly, you can let someone get ahead of you in a line. Such instances can also open doors for small talk.

Here are a few examples:

"It looks like you have been standing for a while now. Why don't you take my seat? I will be hopping off on the next circle."

"Looks like you have been waiting for quite a long time. You can get your cart cleared first. I can wait."

Strike Up Conversations With Strangers

It's not so strange to talk to strangers. In fact, it's really fun. You never know how a random conversation with a stranger can add richness to your day, and comfort the other person if they are in distress. You can talk to your fellow passenger on a bus, your hairstylist, dentist, or a dog walker in a park.

Here are some ideas:

As you remark, "Looks like you travel on the same bus every day." The other person replies, "Oh yes, I do. I work in a supermarket.

The last few days have been really tough for me. I need to go to work even though I have been ill for a while." To which you can respond by saying, "I can understand. You do look tired. But I am sure you will be okay soon. I hope you talk to your supervisor today and they let you go on a break."

In another circumstance, you can start conversing with your hairstylist by saying, "You have really transformed me. Look at me!" "You look fabulous," replies the hairstylist. You can respond by saying "Thanks so much! How do you make it happen?"

It's always good to show concern, empathy, appreciation, and a sense of wonderment to people.

Talk to At Least Five People at Your Workplace

If you are a professional and spend a great deal of time in the office, make it your goal to initiate small talk with at least five people every day; they could be anybody—the office boy, the person who sits next to you, the cashier at the cafeteria, or even your supervisor. Just do it!

Here are a few office small talk ideas to help you get started:

"How has your day been so far?"

"My day has been kind of slow. How about yours?"

"What have you got for lunch?"

"Would you like to grab a cup of coffee?"

"How have you been? I haven't seen you for a while."

As you continue to practice small talk in your everyday life, you will get more conversation ideas. You will soon realize it's not such a big deal to talk to people.

CHAPTER 7: THE ART OF DEALING WITH DIFFERENT TYPES OF PEOPLE

Small talk can pacify even the most difficult of people. Such is the power of saying the right thing at the right moment. But not everybody is born with the gift of gab. Most of us learn it with patience, observation, and experience. Therefore, it's valuable to be in a position where you need to push yourself out of your comfort zone, at least once in a while.

When we come across different types of people with different personalities, backgrounds, and beliefs, we get a chance to grow as an individual. Some people are absolutely delightful. They make your day by just being around, while some people radiate negative vibes. You may find it even harder to make small talk with someone who's simply not interested in talking to you. However, there are situations when you need to connect with people who are not so easy to get along with.

So how do you deal with different personalities and initiate conversations smoothly?

Remember Conversation Ideas

The best way to deal with people who are not like you is to keep some conversation ideas handy and not be too spontaneous (refer to chapter 4). It's better to plan and practice in your head what to say as you meet them. However, don't come across as obviously rehearsed. Take deep breaths, relax, and rub your hands if you need to. You never know; the conversation with a difficult person might also go really well.

Allow the Other Person to Speak First

The safest bet is to allow the other person to speak first. That way, you will not be in a tough spot. You can easily build up on what the other person talks about and the conversation is likely to flow smoothly. You can add input wherever you feel right.

Stick to Safe Topics

You should be careful about what you talk about with anyone who seems hard to get along with. They might not appreciate everything you say to them. You should always stick to safe topics when you talk to someone for the first time. However, if the other person appears to be difficult, then keep it even safer. Don't mention anything they may be touchy about.

For instance, if the person appears to be too traditional or old-fashioned, don't talk about modern age ideologies or values.

Ignore the Offence

If you feel offended by anything the other person has said, you can simply ignore it and move on to some other topic. You don't have to prove your point to anybody. What you believe is what you believe. You should stick to your own values and ideas without being perturbed by others' opinions. It's often futile to get into arguments and unnecessary quarrels with anybody.

Don't Judge Anyone

Everybody has the right to be their own person, right? You may not like them, you may not want to hang out with them, and that's perfectly fine. But you should not judge anybody no matter what they choose to do and how they live.

Most of us are always prompt about judging others without even trying to know them. It's unfair. It's always easier to like someone when you stop judging them on the basis of their habits, lifestyle, language, or behavior.

Look for Common Ground

The smartest way to reduce friction with a person who's unlike you is to find commonalities. It's always possible to have something in common. Stick to those topics and activities. For instance, you work with a really annoying colleague who you can't see eye to eye with. You two always end up arguing about something or the other. In such a scenario, avoid topics that stir up heated discussions. Instead, bring up something where the two of you agree.

For instance, the two of you may have similar views on the company's employee benefit policy; discuss that with each other instead of touching the hot-button issues.

Remember You Can't Please Everybody

You should do your best to be a likeable and amicable person. However, you should never lick somebody's boot. There will always be people who will never like you, no matter how nicely you behave with them. So don't try too hard. Draw your own boundaries. Respect yourself.

Everybody teaches you something, so learn your lessons gracefully. It's not possible to always have pleasant people around. You are bound to meet a lot of weird people, too. So take it in your stride.

CHAPTER 8: TOPICS TO AVOID FOR SMALL TALK

The purpose of small talk is to make the other person feel comfortable. It's meant to bridge the gap between strangers in scenarios where they are put together. Therefore, it's important that what you talk about is carefully thought out. Small talk should be light-hearted, friendly, and completely inoffensive. It should be in no way intrusive in nature.

There are certain topics you should keep at bay when it comes to small talk. You don't want to say anything to upset the person you are perhaps meeting for the first time. It's better to stick to safe topics (refer to earlier chapters).

Here are a few topics you should avoid for small talk -

Personal Finances

You should never ask someone about their personal finances, at least when you meet them for the first time. It's totally inappropriate to ask somebody how much money they make, their investment strategies, and other financial plans. Finances are too personal a topic for strangers to discuss, and even for people who aren't too close. It may make the other person feel awkward, or worse, they might be put off and not want to stay in the conversation.

Neither should you ask them about their finances nor should you offer any financial advice, even if you are tempted to.

Personal Choices

You should never ask someone about their personal life choices —whether they are married or not, their sexual orientation, their cultural beliefs, or their value system. Such topics are extremely personal and maybe complicated for a lot of people. Thus, you should not intrude on your conversation partner's privacy. Small talk is meant to be completely unobtrusive.

Religion

You should avoid talking about religion or faith. It's a sensitive topic and it should not be discussed casually, since everybody has such varied viewpoints about religion that it can offend people easily. So, it's best to keep this topic locked in a box.

Politics

Nobody wants to talk about politics when they want to make small talk. It's not an appropriate topic for two people to connect. People usually have very strong political opinions and it's best to keep opinions out of the picture when you are trying to be genial with somebody.

Sex

You don't want to talk about sex when you are trying to break the ice with a stranger, or even with somebody you are slightly familiar with. You should not even crack coarsely sexual jokes on such occasions. You need to keep in mind that different people have different value systems in regards to sex, which is why it's not an appropriate topic to talk about in a formal environment.

Death or Illness

You don't want to talk about anything unpleasant when you are trying to have a friendly chat with somebody. Of course, you can mention about your own illness if you haven't been doing well lately. However, you don't need to get deep into discussing diseases or death.

Weird Topics That Nobody Is Interested in Talking About

It makes no sense to talk about topics that interest nobody else but you. When you make an effort to chat with somebody casually, let it be about the other person. So don't talk about topics that are too offbeat, or too hard to understand.

For instance, don't start talking about unusual scientific discoveries, historic traditions, or futuristic technologies that not many people know about.

Past Relationships

It's absolutely out of place to talk about your past relationships when you are meeting somebody for a potential romantic association, or to ask the other person about it. You should avoid it, as the other person might get totally offended, and you may miss out on a chance to have a new relationship.

Topics Such as Crime, Famine, Divorce, etc.

You should avoid all sorts of serious topics like crime, famine, divorce, or anything that could upset somebody. Such topics are meant for group discussions or debates. When you meet somebody for the first time, the idea is to lighten up and find common ground with the other person.

Let your small talk be easy, kind, and positive. Remember, small talk is not meant for heated debates or serious discussions of any kind.

CHAPTER 9: SMALL TALK MISTAKES TO AVOID

You want to come across as pleasant and easy to get along with when you initiate small talk with someone. Your attitude could make or break it. What you say is just one aspect of it, the other important aspect is how you behave. There are certain behaviors that are not appropriate and may put off the other person.

Apart from remembering conversation ideas, you should also keep your attitude in check and not do anything, even unknowingly, which might turn the conversation insipid or sour.

The first thought to clench close to your heart when you set out to meet somebody new is that you should feel good about it. Take it as a privilege to meet somebody new and not as a burden. Don't try to get over it as quickly as possible. Be genuine about it and respect it.

Here's what you should not do to mess up your small talk -

Check Your Phone Most of the Time

Some people are just not able to leave their phone alone, which is a bad habit especially when you are talking to somebody. When you are in a conversation, your attention should be focused on the person and not on your phone screen. The person should not feel as if you are not interested in talking to them. So you need to put your phone on airplane mode or simply put it away.

Try to Overpower a Conversation or Win an Argument

Allow the other person to speak, and you be the one who listens. Never interrupt while the person is saying something. Always wait for a thought to end. People who are talkative may get tempted to overpower the conversation with no bad intention. But it's not the right behavior. You should let the other person finish sentences, support their thoughts, and take the conversation ahead in a gentle manner. Don't show your disagreement blatantly or try to win an argument.

You can respond in a polite manner when you don't agree with something - "I see what you are saying, but I had a different experience with it."

Being Dull or Disinterested

Don't appear dull or disinterested. Instead, be curious to know the other person. Show some enthusiasm. You should exude positive energy which should stir up the other person's interest in talking to you. It's a give and take deal. You can't expect the other person to like you unless you don't show some energy and enthusiasm while talking to them.

Say Things That Might Belittle Your Conversation Partner

Some people don't realize it, but they end up saying things that might hurt the other person. When you don't know your conversation partner too well, you should be careful about making comments about their profession, choice of cars, or food preferences. For instance, if the other person talks about the kind of cars they like to drive, you should listen respectfully even if you think they have poor knowledge of cars. You should never belittle (even unknowingly) anyone's choice or knowledge about things.

Pretend or Fake It Too Much

Small talk may be superficial, but it's not really fake. You should be yourself and extend your genuine warmth. If you try to be somebody you are not, sooner or later the mask will drop off and it will be really embarrassing. It's always more charming and endearing to be your own self. People eventually like others who are authentic and honest.

Sound Interrogative

It's good to ask questions, as it will show your interest in the other person; however, don't ask too many questions. The other person will not appreciate it if you sound interrogative. Nobody likes to be put on the spot. Your questions should just persuade someone to talk, then it should flow naturally. There should not be 'questions' fired on the opposite side. There should not be any uncomfortable moments.

Not Responding to Positive Vibes

It would be extremely unwise to ignore somebody's positive vibes. If somebody is being nice to you (smiling at you, offering you a seat, or giving the right signals), you should take it instantly. You should be the one who's always willing to talk, share ideas and thoughts. Most of the crackling conversations happen when people respond to positive vibes.

Force a Sense of Humor

It's good to be funny and crack a joke or two, but trying to be funny in a fabricated manner is not appreciated at all. Don't try to force humor in your conversation, as it may not be taken well by your conversational partner. You should be authentic in your behavior, and not try to put on a persona that's not yours.

As far as humor is concerned, never try to make fun of people or belittle anyone in any way.

Talking All About Yourself

Don't be somebody who just can't see things beyond them. Never ever talk just about yourself! It's an absolutely nasty thing to do. Of course, you can talk about yourself after you have allowed the other person to tell a bit about themselves, and you have responded in a supportive manner. However, a monologue about your achievements, talents, and intelligence is a turn off.

Give Close-Ended Answers to Open-Ended Questions

When someone is trying to be chatty with you and trying to know you, don't be stingy by giving close-ended answers. For instance, if someone asks you, "How was your week?" don't just say it was okay and then move away. Instead, take time to answer in a genuine manner, "It was good. I was able to finish most of my tasks. It was a bit tiring, though." And then ask in return, "How about yours? Looks like you had a hectic one, too."

Avoiding the above conversation behaviors can help you master your social skills.

CHAPTER 10: HOW TO MAKE SMALL TALK MEANINGFUL AND BUILD LASTING CONNECTIONS

Small talk is the first step toward knowing somebody. All sorts of relationships you garner in life are built on the foundation of small talk. When you meet a person for the first time, you knock on their doors with a warm smile, a glint in your eyes, and an affable greeting. That's just the beginning of a possible lasting connection. You can either let the association wane in the first meeting or you can allow it to turn into a relationship.

Whether it's your spouse, best friend, or a dear neighbor, all of them were strangers to you at one point. It's the commonalities and the authenticity of the two people that connect them for life. Hence, you should value small talk and consider it a privilege to meet people.

No matter how awkward, boring, or undesirable small talk may seem, it can make rewarding connections in the long run. It's like if you ignore the opportunity to make small talk with somebody, you may miss out on a good friendship, a solid marriage, or a prolific professional association.

Follow Up After Your First Meeting

Small talk is not always meant for just one meeting. Sometimes you should make efforts to follow up with the person and try to see if the other person is interested in keeping in touch with you. Look out for possibilities.

Some people make the mistake of hesitating to call or message somebody they have met once. They shy away from taking the association forward because of thoughts like "What if they didn't like me?" "Should I call first?" "I won't call till I hear from them," or "It would be embarrassing to message them."

It's not wise to make assumptions and lose out on potential connections—whether they are personal or professional. Relationships of any kind add value to your life; therefore, you should take small talk seriously.

Here are a few instances of how you should follow up with somebody who you have met only once -

"Hey, hope you are doing well. Just wanted to check if you'd like to attend the comedy night this weekend?"

"It was great meeting you yesterday. Let's stay in touch. I'll be going wine-tasting next weekend. Do let me know if you'd like to join."

"I really enjoyed our meeting. I'll keep you posted on my plans to upgrade my website. If I decide to change it, I'd like to give the job to you."

The idea is to make your follow ups more meaningful and substantial.

Add Value to the Other Person's Life

When you take interest in knowing somebody, listen to what they say, support their thoughts, and add appropriate input, it adds value to their life. Communication is a powerful medium to enhance your life in so many ways—you don't just build your network, but also improve your own interpersonal skills.

You get a chance to step out of your comfort zone and experience the world from different viewpoints. That's how you add value to your own life. If you look at things from a broader perspective, everything we want to achieve or gain eventually is an outcome of some sort of communication that happens at some point in time.

You should always remember people you meet, so you can recommend them to people who might need them. For instance, you meet a writer at a party and you know a friend who needs somebody to write for their magazine. You have an opportunity to connect the two. So, don't let your small talk be limited to just a casual chat. Make it more valuable by knowing the other person really well.

Be Available for Help and Advice

You should be the kind of person who's always there for any kind of help and advice. Don't be friendly just on the surface. Let the other person know what you are genuinely capable of. For instance, if you know a great deal about the stock market, let your knowledge be of some help to people who know you. Don't be somebody who brags about their expertise, but never helps or guides others.

Nurture your connections by being there for people who need your expertise in a particular field.

Be Open to Deeper Connections

Some people are just not open to new friendships. They don't want to make deep connections with anybody—regularly keep in touch, meet often, share thoughts and ideas, or reach out for help.

While it's not advisable to deepen your connection with everybody you meet, you should pick and choose at least a few people for long lasting relationships. Take initiatives to make phone calls, set appointments, and meet people over coffee. Don't be afraid to make new friends, even if you feel they might betray or hurt you. It's okay to be betrayed and learn a lesson or two than to be alone.

Put the Other Person First

One of the most endearing qualities to have as a person is to always put others first—listen sincerely to what they say, take initiative to call first, make time according to their schedule, and offer help whenever needed. Of course, you don't want to be sweet and kind to someone who doesn't care to reciprocate. The right person is going to value you and count you amongst their closest friends.

Don't Be Judgmental

Nobody likes to be judged for who they are and how they choose to live. Never ever judge anybody if you want them to stay connected to you. Friendships are free of judgements. So keep it that way. Don't try to be idealistic or preachy.

You can always offer advice or share instances of something having a bad outcome, but don't impose your views on people. Let them fall and get up on their own.

Be Proactive. Keep Commitments

If you want to have a lasting connection with somebody, make it a point to be proactive. Don't wait for the other person to make the first move. Yes, of course, if the other person is not interested in being friends with you, stop right there.

Nonetheless, proactiveness and commitment are essential to be able to nurture a friendship. Don't keep changing, delaying, or canceling appointments.

Spend More Time Together

After you have met a person at somebody's house and both of you realize you hit it off really well, then take it forward and plan more time together. Invite them for coffee, or maybe dinner. Give yourself a chance to explore the association further—talk about more intimate topics, such as love, relationships, personal goals, and beliefs. You never know it may go to a new level and you may find a great friend for life.

Spending time together and getting to know each other is necessary for any relationship—be it romantic or platonic.

Some people are meant to come and go in your life, while some are meant to last a lifetime. You should always be open to meeting people, talking to them, and building your network, as that's the key to an enriched life.

CHAPTER 11: HOW TO FIND OPPORTUNITIES TO MEET NEW PEOPLE

The more people you meet, the better you will get at small talk. We all have different lives. While some of us get to meet new people quite often and easily, some of us don't get many such opportunities. But that does not mean we should not find ways to meet new people. There are plenty of places where you can connect to all sorts of people.

Meeting people is like medicine for your mind and soul. You can live a perfect life by doing all the right things—eating well, sleeping for a sufficient number of hours, exercising, meditating, exploring new places, learning new skills, enjoying your work, being productive, spending your money right, doing charity, and all sorts of good things. But, if you are not socializing, making new friends, and exchanging thoughts and views, there's something valuable missing in your life.

You have to be social to be able to live your life in a wholesome manner. In fact, when you meet a variety of people, you get a chance to rediscover yourself. There are many aspects about your own self that remain under wraps until somebody makes you uncover it. Therefore, you should be intentional about meeting new people. Well, you don't have to go everywhere and be friends with everyone. You need to find places that suit your personality, lifestyle, ideologies, likes, and dislikes.

You may be a working professional or a homemaker, a student or a retired person, an extrovert or an introvert; you can still go out and find your kind of people to interact with.

Join a Place of Common Interest and Activity

The best places to rub shoulders with people are health clubs, dance classes, dog parks, libraries, churches, movie theatres, art galleries, music clubs, and cultural clubs. You should choose a place that matches your interest to find your kind of people. For instance, if you are into fitness, join a gym where you will bump into people who like to stay fit like you. Joining such activity or interest driven places helps you meet people with commonalities, which will ease the effort of making small talk.

Do Some Bar and Restaurant Hopping

Would you like to appear as the outgoing type? Then be seen at bars and restaurants sipping away your favorite cocktail and eating your favorite food. You will find lots of opportunities to approach (or to be approached by) some of the coolest people in town. Get that stunning dress out of your closet and get ready to roll!

Get Associated With a Charitable Organization

Get your noble act together and do some charity! Be part of a charity you believe in and be actively involved in it. Don't just donate some money and remain anonymous about it. Instead, be out there and let people know you for your charitable deeds. Participate in voluntary works, support the active campaigns, and express your views about the cause. Well, the idea is not to brag about it, but to connect with people who have ideas similar to yours.

Participate in Local Activities

Go on a city heritage walk, local brewery tour, or a farmer's market. Such activities connect you to people who appreciate the same kind of things you do. You are more likely to make friends who you can hang out with quite often because you will have a lot of common interests to pursue together.

Meet People in Your Travels

Your fellow travelers could become your lifelong friends. Travel opens up so many opportunities for meaningful conversations and friendships. It also makes you fearless and gives you the ability to trust strangers. You learn to value people who are from different communities and backgrounds, and how they make your travels so memorable for you—drivers, travel agents, waiters, hotel attendants, airline staff, tourist guides, and the folks at the ticket counters in various places. Everybody contributes to your trip; that's why it's nice to remember them and possibly keep in touch with them.

Invite People Home

Host a small party at your place and invite people who are not your close friends. Invite your office acquaintances, neighbors, and somebody who you met lately. Give yourself a chance to be a congenial host. Let your hair down. Play some cool party games. Sip some wine, laugh, dance, go down memory lane and share a few anecdotes—let your quirky side be seen.

Connect With New People on Social Media

You can connect with a lot of fun and interesting people on social media. In fact, it's one of the best ways to discover new friends without going anywhere! Social media is a cool and easy platform, even for introverts, because you can engage with all sorts of people from behind a mobile phone screen. You can reach out to as many people as possible. There is literally no limit to how many people you can connect with on social media (more about it in chapter 12).

Attend Seminars (and Webinars)

The best way to upgrade your knowledge and expertise on a subject is to attend relevant seminars (and webinars), and also meet an array of intellectual people. You will get a chance to overcome your social fears and improve your small talk abilities. The benefit of attending such events is you don't have to ooze charm or be witty. You can simply focus on the topic of the seminar and share your views about it.

Don't Skip Events Like Festivals, Weddings, and Baby Showers

Every event opens doors for enriched conversations and rewarding associations. If you are someone who enjoys celebrations, family love, and lots of mush, always be available to attend events like cultural festivals, weddings, and baby showers to be able to connect to people on a more personal level. You get to feel a range of emotions on such occasions, which is essential for your mental and emotional wellbeing.

Banks, Hospitals, Schools, and Supermarkets

You meet people at places like banks, hospitals, veterinary clinics, schools, salons, and supermarkets—these are places where you need to go once in a while. You may not intend to talk to people at such places without reason, but you sure have the opportunity to meet all kinds of people.

For instance, if you are attending your child's parents-teacher conference at their school, it's highly likely for you to bump into other parents who you would like to exchange some thoughts about the education system, your childrens' progress, or possibly discuss a few common academic challenges.

There's no dearth of opportunities to meet new people and form new friendships as long as you are willing to take the social plunge.

CHAPTER 12: HOW TO MEET NEW PEOPLE ON SOCIAL MEDIA

The digital world is a blessing for socially challenged people. If you cringe at the thought of meeting new people in the real world, you can at least connect with people in the virtual world. You don't have to smile, make eye contact, or have great body language to do that. You should harness the power of social media and make friends online.

The best part about connecting with new people on social media is you don't have any kind of pressure to deal with. You don't have to worry about people's perception of you, how you dress, or what you say or do.

Social media is the best place to make professional connections which could possibly help you grow in your career. You also get lots of like-minded people to meet online who have similar interests, beliefs, and needs as yours. For instance, if you are a passionate traveler, you will find many people on social media who are as passionate about travel as you. It's fun to exchange travel stories and inspire each other.

Let Your Profile Picture Say it all

The first step you take toward reaching out to people on social media, be it on any platform, is to put up a nice profile picture of yourself. You should be smiling in the picture, so people who don't know you personally may find you approachable. A smile is the window to a person's heart. So appear to be pleasant, friendly, and warm in your picture.

Please don't put a picture of your dog as your display picture. The more authentic and personal your profile appears, the better it is.

Send Connection Requests

Get rid of your social media inhibitions and be open to sending connection requests to as many people as possible. However, keep in mind it should not be done in an aggressive way. You have to do it in a respectful manner. Reach out to people who are in your niche, or who are part of your common friend list.

For instance, if you are into fitness and yoga, reach out to people who would like to be similarly updated. On the contrary, if you post a lot about technology and gadgets, don't connect with people who like jewellery. There has to be relevance.

Accept Friend Requests

Be open to accepting friend requests. However, be careful about who you connect with. There are many fake accounts on social media you should stay away from. Also, if you are someone in your 30s or 40s, don't accept friend requests from teenagers who're just trying to be around for no real purpose.

Share Updates About Your Life

Don't be inactive after creating your social media profile. Make efforts to keep your account active. While there are so many social media channels available, you don't have to be on each one of them, unless you want to promote your business. Pick just one or two social media channels and try to keep them updated.

The best way to grow your visibility on social media and reach more people is to share regular life updates—you went on a vacation, celebrated your birthday, moved into a new house, had a baby, or bought a new car. Whatever it is, just share it with your network. However, don't share anything and everything. Keep all the mundane, not-so-interesting, or too personal stuff private. For instance, don't share pictures of you buying groceries or visiting a doctor.

Like, Share, and Comment on Others' Posts

Engage with other people's posts, too. Check out what they are up to. It's your chance to make small talk with them in the virtual world, which is easier than in the real world. Don't just scroll through your feed, but make it a point to like, share, and comment on posts you enjoy. For instance, if you like baking, follow content on baking and that's how you will get a chance to engage with people who enjoy baking just like you.

Social media allows you to connect with people who have similar interests as yours. It's your place to find commonalities and grow into a community.

Don't Be Fake

Just like in the real world where you meet people physically, you are appreciated more if you are genuine and honest. Similarly, you are admired more when you are relatable, even in the digital world. Don't try to project yourself as somebody who you are not. For instance, if you are an intellectual person in the real world, let your posts reflect the same in the digital world, too. Don't try to act silly just for the sake of appearing cool, as that might not go too well with the people who follow you.

Be Genuinely Interested in People

Don't engage with people just for the sake of it. Be genuinely interested in what they do and who they are. Be observant and thoughtful. For instance, if somebody has posted about the latest book they have enjoyed reading, ask questions about the book. Don't just stick to generic comments like "Oh, that is awesome!" Instead, write specific stuff, such as "I have never read a book by this author, but now I will pick up the book that you recommend. I have been craving to read something meaningful and inspiring for quite sometime now."

Long, thoughtful, and specific comments help you gain more visibility on social media.

Send Direct Messages

When you reach a point where you notice somebody engages on your updates quite a lot, and you have kind of developed a liking for the person, you should take the next step and send them a direct message. However, don't be intrusive or personal with your messages. Just send across a friendly message that indicates a positive vibe from you.

For instance, you can write, "Hey, we have been engaging on each other's posts for a while now. I really appreciate what you do. I always look forward to your updates. Keep up the good work!" Wait for the other person's response. If they are interested in knowing you, they will reply, or else you can simply move on.

Appreciate What Others Are Doing

Show your constant appreciation about what others are doing. Social media tells you all about people's lives. If somebody has got a promotion, acknowledge it and congratulate them on their success. If somebody has started a new business, encourage them with your kind words. The more you support people in the virtual world, the better image you will build for yourself. It becomes a society based on mutual admiration over a period of time, which helps everybody.

Stay Away From Negativity

Social media can get quite ugly sometimes. You need to guard yourself and stay away from any sort of negativity. Never be part of any futile arguments or heated discussions. Never put up a post to bring somebody down. It doesn't go very well on social media. You may get attention for some time, but it quickly ruins your reputation. People are wary of connecting with somebody who is negative, critical, or generally unpleasant.

Plan to Meet Offline

Social media can be a great place to foster friendships and rela-tionships. There are a lot of good people on social media who could add value and beauty to your life. You should plan to meet at least some of them offline as well. You can find friends for life, your love interest, even your professional counterparts.

Be open to new associations on social media. It's the best medium to turn into an outgoing, confident, and likeable person.

CHAPTER 13:
HOW TO END A
CONVERSATION WELL

It's important to make a graceful exit from a conversation and not leave it abruptly or awkwardly in any given situation. You could be at a professional networking event, a friend's birthday party, a family gathering, or in a hotel lobby; ending a conversation smartly and politely with a tacit promise of another meeting is part of mastering small talk.

The last part of a chat or rendezvous hints toward a long lasting connection. Effective communication involves all aspects of the chat—the beginning, the middle, and the end.

If you don't end it right, the effort of small talk may fall flat and you don't want that, right? So keep in mind the following tips and ways to end it right -

Make Polite Statements

When you feel the conversation is waning, grab the opportunity to end it in a polite manner by saying, "It was lovely meeting you, let's keep in touch." If the other person continues to talk, listen to them for a while. However, if you have other plans and you want to leave, indicate that without interrupting.

Wait for a pause from the other side and then say -

"I am so glad we met. Let's catch up again sometime."

"It was great talking to you. Let's plan to meet again sometime."

Offer Your Business Card

Giving away your business card, or asking for one, is also a smart way to conclude a conversation. You can tell the person while handing over your card that they are welcome to contact you anytime.

For example, "Here's my card for you to get in touch whenever you'd like to." After you have given your card, you can say, "I'll see you soon."

Look at Your Watch or Phone

If you feel the conversation is flowing quite smoothly and the end doesn't seem close, you should mention time. You can indicate you'd like to leave by looking at your watch or checking your phone. You can say, "I am getting late for another appointment. It was lovely meeting you. Let's catch up sometime soon."

Move Toward the Door Slowly

You can start walking toward the door slowly and say something like - "My boyfriend is waiting for me in the lobby. I need to rush. I enjoyed our conversation a lot. Let's connect again sometime."

By making a physical movement of heading outside, you can break the chain of thoughts politely and end the chat for the day.

Mention Something You Want to Do

If you're at a party, there are quite a few ways to conclude the conversation -

"I'll go and fill my glass. It's been a pleasure talking to you."

"I need to use the restroom. It was lovely chatting with you."

"I have to meet some other friends over there (perhaps wave at some people). I'll see you again."

Slip Through the Lulls

You can also take advantage of the pauses after a topic has been discussed for a while and there's nothing more to talk about it. For instance, the other person says, "Well...it looks like everybody is enjoying the evening," you can quickly add, "Yeah, right. It was lovely, indeed. It was great meeting you. I have to go now."

Introduce Them to Somebody Else

Another good way to exit a conversation is to introduce the other person to somebody else you know at the gathering. You can say to them, "May I introduce you to a friend who is also into digital marketing? Perhaps you can talk to them about your new project." Then, you can let the two talk while you take your leave.

Mention Your Other Plans

You can politely mention your other plans for the day and take your leave. For instance, you can say, "I need to pick up my kids from school. I'll be leaving in a bit. Let's catch up sometime next week." That way, you will not offend them and you are more likely to connect again.

You Can Walk Toward Food

You can ask the other person if they would like to check out the buffet, and if they decline the invitation, you have successfully concluded the conversation. If they are also ready to eat, you can chat a bit more, then begin to mingle with other people, providing you an opportunity to bid goodbye to the person.

Go Back to What You Talked About

You can end your conversation by summing up what you talked about. It's a great way to make the other person feel you really listened and absorbed what they shared with you. For instance, if they told you about preparing for an event, mention something like, "I hope you have a great event; I'd love to know how it went. It was good talking with you about behind-the-scenes stories of the event."

Thank the Person, Say Something Kind

Showing your gratitude and saying something kind on purpose are also polite ways of ending a conversation. You can say things like -

"Thank you so much for sharing your experiences. I really enjoyed talking with you."

"I am happy I ran into you. Thanks for your time."

"I really appreciate your guidance. I'll keep your suggestions in mind while buying my car."

Remember, ending a conversation on the right note is as import-ant as its beginning. To keep in touch with the people you initiate small talk with, avoid abrupt or rude interruptions to flowing conversations.

CHAPTER 14: HOW TO GROW AS AN INDIVIDUAL

Growth is an integral part of life. Just as you nurture a small child or plant, your inner being also needs to grow daily. You can never really say you have grown enough, or learned everything. There's always more to learn and more to explore. Some of us are born a certain way with certain attributes, while some of us need to learn certain things.

Not everybody is naturally people-friendly or outgoing. Some of us want to run out of situations where we need to encounter people, talk to them, and be nice and friendly with them. Nonetheless, the truth is it's people who teach us a great deal about life. People actually enrich us, so we should not run away from them.

It's up to us whether we want to learn and enrich ourselves, or remain where we are. While we try to become better individuals, it's important to remember we are amazing the way we are. Not everybody is meant to be social, outgoing, and charismatic. Introverts also add their own value to people's lives. Everybody has different roles to play. Therefore, we should not imitate anybody. That would be a disrespect to our very own self.

Be Aware of Your Surroundings

The ideal thing to do is observe your surroundings—the people, circumstances, situations, and environments. The more you learn and filter, the better human being you will become. You need to take the best of all that is happening around you and leave everything negative.

For instance, the people in your office are being spiteful and cruel for no reason. They are all kicking up a fuss and scheming against each other. What should you do? You can simply be aware of it, and be at peace. You don't have to react, or try to change anything. You just have to be your positive self.

Celebrate Your Uniqueness

While you learn and grow as an individual, you also need to celebrate your uniqueness. You need to believe you are an awesome human being and are born to make a difference. Being confident of who you are and taking full charge of your thoughts, words, and actions can ease so much for you.

While you have learned so far that small talk can be mastered with practice, and remembering some conversation ideas, you should also understand that developing conversation skills is also a matter of growing as an individual. Many people don't realize only a good person can communicate effectively. If you don't think right, or feel right, about other people, you cannot really connect with them either.

Have the Right Attitude Toward Learning

The right attitude plays a key role in mastering your social skills. You don't have to do it in the spirit that you *have* to do it because everybody else does it, and that's what is acceptable by the world at large. On the contrary, you should do it in the spirit that it's *your* personal journey, and you want to be the best person you can be in any given situation—you want to reach out to people and be nice to them.

Whatever you try to accomplish or achieve in life should be done with the proper intent and purpose. You should not try to be like everybody else. Why should you lose your true self in the wake of learning something? The worst mistake you can ever make is forgetting or stifling your own self. Therefore, it's important to remember the purpose behind your goals in life.

You may have a simple goal, like mastering small talk. However, you should know why you would like to master it. Is it because you think you want to be like other people, or is it because you think you lack those skills and you want to acquire them? There's a difference.

You should always work toward acquiring new skills—the skills you need to become a more refined individual.

Don't Envy Anyone

You should also realize people who have magnetic personalities also have their share of weaknesses, insecurities, and fears. Nobody is as perfect or happy as they appear. Everybody struggles in some area or another. You will be surprised to know many people you envy for their outgoing personas could be timid from inside.

The point is, you should be happy with who you are, and get rid of any false notions you may have about yourself, or people in general.

Read Good Books, Watch Good Stuff Online

Reading good books and watching good online videos are also great ways to learn new things. You should always be looking out for upgrading your skills. There are plenty of online courses available these days—you can pick and choose the ones which suit you.

The idea is to constantly work on your personal growth.

You should also keep an eye on various events that take place, where you get a chance to hear from industry experts and brush up your knowledge on a particular subject. As things are getting more and more digital these days, you should use the medium for self-development.

So to sum up, you need to do the following to grow as an individual -

- Appreciate people and learn from them.
- Take charge of your thoughts, words, and actions.
- Accept yourself the way you are. You should celebrate your uniqueness.
- Be aware of your intent and purpose behind acquiring certain skills.
- Being a nice person goes a long way. Be honest and authentic. Don't fake it too much.
- Keep upgrading your skills through books, online videos, and courses.
- Understand that people who project themselves as confident and outgoing also have flaws.

The journey of growing into a great personality isn't easy, though. It comes with its own share of challenges and roadblocks. Be prepared to feel overwhelmed, disappointed, and dejected once in a while. You will not always have the energy to think right and do right. You will not always get the best of people and circumstances to deal with. You will not get the cushion you need. There will be many situations where you will be ignored, sidelined, mistreated, and even bad mouthed.

Well, you should allow yourself to take some time off and hide in your own shell—to restore your spirits. You will get the strength to bounce back and elevate your spirits!

The biggest strength of a good person is they never stoop down to bad things. They choose their own happiness, their own adventure, and stay the course.

CHAPTER 15: WHY IS SELF-LOVE NECESSARY AND HOW TO PRACTICE IT

Loving yourself is key to becoming a confident person. You can't make others love you if you don't love yourself in the first place. Self-love is as essential for your being as anything else. Most people are not able to understand self-love. They think self-love is being selfish or self-centered. People also think that self-love is some kind of a lunatic behavior.

So what is self-love?

Self-love is taking care of yourself. It's being mindful of your happiness, dreams, and desires. It's listening to your heart. It's eating well, taking sufficient rest, engaging in physical activities, enjoying a good social life, and doing things you enjoy.

When you love yourself, you take care of yourself and also pamper yourself once in a while. Self-love keeps you sane. In today's stressful world, it's easy to lose your mental balance and feel emotionally low. Thus, you should lighten up on your own. Don't wait for anyone else to make you feel good. It's your own responsibility to take care of your mental and emotional wellbeing.

Self-love helps you connect with others in a healthy way. You want to connect with others not because you are scared of being alone, but because you want to live a rewarding life. The more people you have in your life, the more experiences you garner and more energy you exude.

People who love themselves are naturally happy and positive people, which makes them more approachable. They are able to have richer conversations, make friends easily, and build better relationships in the long run.

How to Practice Self-Love

Before you practice self-love, it's important to be aware of its value. Don't think of it as something optional, rather as something vital to your wellbeing. The moment you realize its value, you will learn the ways to love yourself.

Don't Be Harsh on Yourself

Most people are unforgiving to themselves. They feel guilty about everything they do. They can't get over their mistakes. They end up spending most of their lives being guilty about nothing. Such people allow others to overpower them, which is totally unfair.

So stop being harsh on yourself and learn to forgive and forget your mistakes. Unburden any thought from your heart that makes you feel sorry for yourself.

When you harbor too much guilt and unforgiveness in your heart, whether it's for yourself or others, it keeps you from being your real self and building relationships.

Be in Good Company

Avoid people who have nothing good to say or do. Surround yourself with good people—progressive, kind, and thoughtful people. Good people radiate positivity and rub off their goodness on others. For instance, if you stay with somebody who's intellectual, you will begin to develop your own intellect within you.

The more positivity and uplifting atmosphere you have around, the happier you will become. Being in the company of good people is part of self-care.

Learn to Say 'No'

Don't be a 'yes' person all the time. If you never say no to people, they are going to take you for granted. They will consider you available for anything, anytime. Once you have set a certain image of you in their minds, it will not change easily. Therefore, you should not make people have unreasonable expectations from you.

You should know your limitations, preferences, and priorities. Give priority to your own health, needs, and plans. Never ignore or undervalue your own things for the sake of others.

Take Time Off Once in a While

Don't be a workaholic or someone who's always seen taking care of the house, running errands, or picking groceries. It's good to love your work or be particular about keeping your house in order. However, being too busy or occupied all the time is not right. You should live a balanced life and allow yourself to take a break once in a while to refresh your energy, put your feet up, and simply do nothing.

Don't Chase Perfection

Everything can't be perfect and you must accept it. Don't run after perfection. It's not worth it. You are far more valuable than your perfect office project. It's absolutely useless to do something perfectly and ruin yourself. Many people get so obsessed about perfection that they lose their mind, and their loved ones, too. People who are too fanatic about achieving perfection in everything they do tend to ignore other more valuable things in life.

Avoid Being a People Pleaser

Don't be somebody who's always worried about people's opinions and thoughts. Just be the good person you are. It's simply not possible to please everybody all the time. Do what you think is right in any given situation. You will upset many people no matter what you do, so why not do what you really want?

Just Relax; Don't Be an Overthinker

People who think too much are never happy. Learn to let your hair down and embrace spontaneity. Don't analyze situations or people too much. Remember, nobody thinks about you too much. So, you should also not give anybody undue importance in your life. Focus on yourself and your growth as an individual.

Appreciate and Reward Yourself

You should give yourself a round of applause for the amazing person you are turning into every day. You should list down all your achievements and successes in a diary and give yourself a pat. Celebrate your little milestones from time to time. Go on a shopping spree, get a nice head massage, or treat yourself with a fantastic dinner at your favorite restaurant.

Take up New Challenges

Self-love is also about taking up new challenges for your betterment. You should push yourself and stretch your limits. For instance, if you want to get into shape, challenge yourself to run for an hour every day. It will be hard for you to run for even fifteen minutes for the first few days, but you will get used to it. If you are consistent at it, you will be able to complete the challenge and discover your own strength.

Let Toxic People Make an Exit From Your Life

If you have certain people in your life who're creating havoc, get rid of them. Don't be the one who eases friction all the time. Don't let your peace be taken away! You should be the one guarding your mental peace. It's better to live your life alone than with someone who's draining you.

Remember, toxic people do you more harm than good. So the best way to live your life is to filter out all the things that are causing you stress.

Nurture Your Passions

Is there anything you love doing a lot—painting, poetry, dancing, or anything artistic? Do it as often as possible. There are people who love different art forms and spend a lot of time pursuing and polishing their skills. Keep doing what you love the most, so you master it.

You should also pursue things that may not be artistic, but you truly enjoy them, such as sports, movies, or travel.

Choose Your Friends Wisely

Although it's good to make small talk with possibly everybody you meet, it's not necessary that you become friends with everybody. In fact, you should choose your friends with care. Focus on quality, rather than quantity. You may have many casual friends, but be particular about who becomes your close friend.

Your friends have a great influence on your life, which is why you should choose them wisely. Don't feel obligated to hang out with somebody you don't get along with.

Begin to love yourself today. You deserve to be loved and cared for.

CHAPTER 16: HOW TO SET BOUNDARIES FOR PEOPLE

All that we have learned so far in this book is about being that outgoing, congenial, and social person who's loved by everybody. However, in this chapter, we will learn how to set boundaries for people. Yes, people are important. You should value each person you have in your life. Show your gratitude to them, be responsive to their needs, and do your best to support them in whatever manner you can. But, don't make the mistake of being unfair to yourself.

Many people are just too meek to ever say no to anyone. They like to be too kind and generous to everybody, on every occasion. It's a kind of an imbalance they live with, and perhaps most of such people are not even aware of it. They do so much for people who don't even value them.

You need to ask yourself a few questions before you shower your kindness and generosity over people - "Why am I doing it? Is it because I don't want to hurt them or am I scared to lose them as friends?"

Most of us end up being people pleasers because of our own incorrect thinking patterns. We have this false notion within our heads that, if we don't do a particular thing for somebody, they will be angry and perhaps exclude us from their circle of friends.

To be a confident individual, it's absolutely vital to guard your own self-worth. You need to rise above your insecurities. You need to learn that people don't like you or want to hang out with you because you please them all the time. People like to be around you for who you are—your personality, the way you talk and express your ideas, the words you use, your viewpoints about life, and your values.

You will always have the right kind of people around as friends, even if you disagree with them on certain things.

When you set boundaries for people, you don't just do a favor to yourself, but also to people in general. People respect and value you more when they understand that you know your worth. They will never take you for granted. They will always know what to expect from you. When you have set your boundaries with people, moments of frustration, misunderstanding, or disappointment are less likely to happen with anybody. And that's how you establish healthy relationships with people where everybody is an equal and nobody is trying to overpower or take undue advantage of somebody's gullibility.

Don't Do Stuff That's Not Part of Your Job

Is your boss asking you to run an errand for them? It's important to set boundaries right from the start at your workplace. Don't let anybody in your office make you do stuff that's not part of your job, or anything that messes with your mental peace, time of rest, or values.

You can say no politely without upsetting them -

"Hey, would you mind picking my groceries from the supermarket on the way?"

"I am afraid I have some other commitments after work. I will be taking a different route home today."

Stick to Your Plans

It's okay to change plans for your friends or the people who you are really close to, but don't do that all the time. If you want to do something for a better lifestyle and health, stick to it. For instance, if you want to wake up early and go for a run, don't change it because somebody wants you to be out really late into the night.

Of course, it's fun to be partying until 2 a.m. However, do it if you want to do it and you are okay about sleeping in the next day. But, if you have been trying to get into a routine of getting up early and building your muscles, then don't let anything or anyone come in the way.

You can decline the invitation by saying, "I'd have loved to come, but I'd rather sleep at 10 p.m. I need to be out of bed by 5 a.m tomorrow."

Be assertive about your plans and agendas.

Don't Feel Obligated to Spend Money

Your friends want you to tag along for a weekend escape to some exotic place and stay in a fancy resort. It's up to you whether you want to pitch in or not. If you decided to save some money for a dream trip and not splurge on weekend getaways, you should let your friends carry on with their plan.

Never allow anyone else to make you spend your money. You can simply tell them, "I have something urgent to finish on the weekend. Maybe next time."

Don't Take the Pressure to Open up

Some people expect you to behave in a certain way—share private details of your life, become too friendly too soon, or meet more often than you would like. Don't take the pressure of getting too close to somebody who you have just met or somebody you don't find too interesting.

You can say things like -

"That is too personal a question. I am afraid I won't be answering that."

"Please excuse me. I have a deadline to meet."

"We can catch up some other day. I need to go now."

Don't Hang Out With People Who Are Always Nasty

You should never hang out with nasty people—the kind of people who always have something negative to talk about, who are mostly ridiculing and frustrating other people. It's of no value to be around such people, as they will rub their nastiness off on you. Either you will become like them or you will stifle your own growth.

Don't tolerate any inappropriate behavior by anyone. If something doesn't feel right, say so and move away.

Do What Makes You Happy and Makes Your Life Better

Whenever you are in a situation where you need to make a decision in terms of what to do, always consider what impact it is going to have on your life. Refrain from doing things that are not good for you, no matter who is telling you to do them. For instance, somebody might tell you to date a person who they think is right for you. But what about you? How do you feel about it? Don't say yes to somebody just out of politeness. Rather give it a good thought and do as your heart says.

You can say, "I really don't think they are my kind of person. I'd rather wait for the right one to come along. I am in no hurry!"

Stay Away From Arguments and Fights

Some people have the habit of arguing and fighting about everything possible. Anything you do or say can upset them or make them question you. They like to get into heated debates on topics that are not even related to them. You have the choice to stay away from such scenarios. Don't feel obligated to give them explanations of any sort.

Unfriend or Block People if You Need To

Today when social media is such an important part of our lives, we need to be aware of its downsides, too. Many people try to poke you, be annoying by sending you non-stop messages, or too much spammy stuff. Stop them right there!

Block people who are outrageously annoying or obnoxious. Unfriend those who you think are not adding any value to your life—they are just being snoopy.

Set healthy boundaries for your wellbeing. Respect your time, body, mind, intellect, and values. Remember, saying no to people doesn't make you a bad person. In fact, by setting your priorities right, and sticking to them, you become a strong and impressive individual who everybody looks up to.

CHAPTER 17: YOU ARE AN AMAZING PERSON AND YOU CONTROL YOUR DESTINY

You are what you believe in. If you believe you are an amazing person and you have control over your destiny, then you truly do. There's a lot that life gives or takes away. However, there's a lot we create for ourselves, and for others. So be sure you create something really awesome.

Most people spend their lives simply envying others. They assume the people around them have fabulous lives—everybody else except them are super confident, smart, and absolutely happy. They don't realize everybody is more or less sailing in the same boat. Nobody is living a perfect life. Yes, some people are great at pretending. Some people have the skills to impress others with their superficial attributes. Even if they are pathetically shallow from within, they have the knack to cover it up with their refined outlook.

The truth is, nobody is enviable. Everybody has lessons to learn, skills to acquire, and regrets to bury. So you should be proud of yourself because you are honest about how you feel and who you are. You are not hiding behind glossy appearances. You are aware of your flaws and that's your biggest strength. You are amazing because you live without pretenses.

People who live pretentious lives never grow. They don't take charge of their lives. Their sole ambition in life is to impress others. However, they forget to discover themselves, their true beliefs, passions, and purposes.

If you are somebody who struggles with your social skills, take a deep breath and smile. Don't be ashamed of your shyness. Be aware that your social skills are just a key to your whole being. You just need to unlock the super power in you!

Your willingness to overcome your weaknesses and learn new skills shows your strength and wisdom.

So here's how you do it -

Design Your Own Life Strategy

Each person should have a larger view of their life. You should know in your heart what kind of life you want to live—what kind of work you want to do, the kind of person you want to marry, the experiences you want to have, the memories you want to create, and the purposes you want to fulfill. Don't be vague about your life.

You should take charge of your life and never go with the flow. Yes, certain things are not in your control. You can't possibly have everything you wish for, or everything the way you want, but you can still take charge of your actions and make conscious choices in life.

Be Aware of Your Thoughts

You lose control of so many things in your life when you are not aware of what you are thinking. Everything begins with your thoughts. When you think right, you say the right things, and act right, too. Unfortunately, most of us don't realize this simple formula of life. If we think of it deeply, we will understand we have such power in our hands, actually in our heads—our thoughts. Our minds direct us into everything we do.

Don't Allow Others to Define You

You are not who people think you are. People may perceive you in a certain way based on what they expected you to be. People are often very quick in forming an opinion, and most of the opinions or perceptions are based on one instance, one conversation, or one meeting. It's not fair to judge or define anybody based on just one instance. Neither should you do that to anybody nor should you allow anybody else to do so to you. Well, you can't stop somebody else from judging you, but you can choose to remain unaffected by it.

Keep Rediscovering Yourself

There's a lot you are born with, and quite a lot you inherit from your parents. And, as you grow up to be an adult, you develop and imbibe a lot from influences around you. We continue to learn through life, knowingly or unknowingly. However, you should also make efforts to rediscover yourself.

Never come to a point when you are completely complacent about your growth or your beauty as a human being. Try new things, have an adventurous soul, and embrace possibilities.

Value Your Relationships

Relationships help you become a better person—you learn to be more tolerant, patient, loving, kind, and forgiving. Imagine a life where you have nobody to deal with, no arguments, no resentments, no tears, no joys, no laughter, and no expectation to meet; such a life will be soulless. Therefore, you should value and nurture your relationships. We tend to take certain relationships for granted because we know they are so strong, but we still need to nurture them.

Boost Your Strengths

Don't be too consumed into working on your weaknesses and sideline your strengths. Be equally aware of strengths, and work toward enhancing them as well. You could be great at doing things independently or encouraging people and uplifting others—these are valuable qualities to have and you should boost them. Let people be aware of these qualities in you and value you more.

One of the gravest mistakes we make is we talk a great deal about our weaknesses in front of others and make them believe so about ourselves. Instead, we should talk (not boast) about our strengths and let them become the ruling force of our lives.

Don't Dig Too Much Into Your Past

If you live in your past, you will miss out on your present. One of the keys to creating a beautiful destiny for yourself is to leave your past behind to live in your present with awareness. Some people keep revisiting their past, which makes them depressed for no reason. You should remind yourself that nobody else except you has the right to judge you for anything. You need to let go of the things that were never meant for you—broken relationships, lost jobs, or missed opportunities.

Be Persistent About Your Dreams and Goals

Only persistent people reach their destinies. Never be over-powered by circumstances or negative remarks from others. Work toward achieving your goals without talking too much about them. You should hold certain dreams and goals close to your heart and not share them with everybody. Be consistent at doing what is required to be able to reach your goals.

You will come across many situations when you will feel like giving up, or you will simply lose your mojo; however, you need to be persistent about your dreams.

Just Keep Learning

Never ever get tired of learning new things. It's a privilege to get to learn and acquire new skills. It's a way of enriching yourself as an individual. Whether it's learning to master small talk, or anything else for that matter, learning is one of the keys to a good life.

And learning doesn't always have to come from books or colleges. You should learn from life circumstances, your own mistakes, and even from other peoples' mistakes.

Never Be Ashamed of Anything About You

To become the person you were born to be, learn to be proud of yourself, never ashamed. Stop comparing yourself with other people—their lives, their spouses, their jobs, and their money. Believe you have the best of everything, and you'll have the power to achieve whatever you set your mind to.

Make Proper Decisions

Correct decisions taken today reward you tomorrow—this is the key point of life. Your decision to invest in your health today will keep you in good shape tomorrow. Make sure all your key decisions in life are well thought out. Never make decisions based on impulse or emotions. Think long term and view life from a broader perspective. Remember, there's nothing more charming than wisdom.

You can design your own destiny, as long as you believe you are an amazing person and were born to be an inspiration.

CONCLUSION

You can become the best version of yourself at any point in your life. It doesn't matter at what age, or stage, you are in. The only thing you need is the fire to be who you want to be. You can become more social and outgoing if you want to. Your life is your story, and you should write it yourself—the kind of life you want to live, the kind of relationships you want to have, and how you want to project yourself to the world.

It doesn't matter if you are an introvert who finds it difficult to mingle with people; you can still develop the skills and gain the confidence to be the kind of person who's liked by everybody.

There are various aspects to being a confident person. It's not just about being outgoing or social. Yes, you can acquire the attributes of a good conversationalist, learn the knack of slipping into a conversation, and making a graceful exit, too. However, to be a confident person on a deeper level, you need to love yourself, which you have learned in this book. You need to grow as an individual, set your priorities right, have the right kind of people in your life, and set healthy boundaries for them.

Your journey of becoming a likeable person begins with recognizing your own true worth, a little time into self-reflection, and then understanding how people are important and how you should go about cultivating long lasting relationships.

You shouldn't just chase people or situations where you are bound to talk. Take it easy and let it come to you naturally. You will get it naturally as long as you have the right attitude—eagerness to meet all kinds of people, curiosity to know them, and sincerity to become a nicer individual.

Now that you have read the book, it's time for you to think of various situations you want to be put in to be able to make small talk with all sorts of people. Take this book as your friend who's available to help and guide you whenever you run out of conversation ideas or you need a little push to keep striving on.

As you go out into the world, don a new perspective that, when you initiate a chat with somebody, it's your way of showing appreciation and acceptance to that person. Enjoy mastering small talk and keep becoming the person you want to be!

REFERENCES

Borenstein, J. (2020, February 12). *Self-Love and what it means.* Brain & Behavior Research Foundation. https://www.bbr-foundation.org/blog/self-love-and-what-it-means

Connell, J. (2018, November). *30 Ways to set boundaries: A guide for people pleasers.* Jasonconnell.co. https://jasonconnell.co/boundaries/

Frost, A. (2019, July 25). *The ultimate guide to small talk: Conversation starters, powerful questions, & more.* Hubspot. https://blog.hubspot.com/sales/small-talk-guide

Hall, J. (2013, August 18). *13 Simple ways you can have more meaningful conversations.* Forbes. https://www.forbes.com/sites/johnhall/2013/08/18/13-simple-ways-you-can-have-more-meaningful-conversations/?sh=331a48944fe9

Hays, J. (2014, August 12). *30 Ways to practice self-love and be good to yourself.* Lifehack. https://www.lifehack.org/articles/communication/30-ways-practice-self-love-and-good-yourself.html

Martha, L. (2013, September 9). *10 Most common mistakes in a conversation.* Lifehack. https://www.lifehack.org/articles/communication/10-most-common-mistakes-conversation.html

Morin, D. A., Wendler, D., & Psy.D. (2020, November 24). *How to not get nervous talking to people (for introverts).* SocialPro. https://socialpronow.com/blog/how-to-never-be-nervous-around-people/

Park, C. (2015, June 2). *An introvert's guide to small talk: Eight painless tips.* Forbes. https://www.forbes.com/sites/christina-park/2015/03/30/an-introverts-guide-to-small-talk-eight-painless-tips/?sh=31ca1d94574a

Pegler, L. (2019, October 20). *The importance of small talk and how to perfect it.* Medium. https://medium.com/swlh/the-import-ance-of-small-talk-and-how-to-perfect-it-5685fb611083

Winch, G. (2020, September 6). *10 Ways to become more likable.* Psychology Today. Www.psychologytoday.com. https://www.psychologytoday.com/us/blog/the-squeaky-wheel/202009/10-ways-become-more-likable

Zetlin, M. (2016, April 29). *11 Graceful ways to end a conversation that work 100 percent of the time.* Inc. https://www.inc.com/minda-zetlin/11-foolproof-ways-to-nicely-end-a-conversation.html

Made in United States
Orlando, FL
30 June 2024

48470896R00059